MEN OF SCIENCE

MEN OF GOD

Great Scientists of the Past Who Believed the Bible

By Henry M. Morris

First printing: 1982
Revised printing: 1988
Fifth printing: July 1990
Tenth printing: May 1994
Fifteenth printing: July 1999

ISBN: 0-89051-080-6
Library of Congress Catalog Number: 82-70271

Cataloging in Publication Data

Morris, Henry Madison, 1918-
Men of science — men of God
Scientists. 2. Religion and science —
History of controversy. I. Title.
509 82-70271

Cover by Marvin Ross

Printed in the United States of America.

CONTENTS

Samuel F. B. Morse • Joseph Henry • Matthew Maury •
James Simpson • James Joule • Adam Sedgwick • William
Whewell • Henry Rogers

INTRODUCTION

Ever since the industrial revolution and the great accomplishments in technology which developed from it, the nations of the world have paid homage to their scientists. "Science" has become almost a magic word. When the eminent scientist, "Dr. Sagacious," speaks on any subject, his word must be accepted as authoritative. If "science" has proved something, then that is that; there is no more room for discussion.

As a matter of fact, scientists do undergo a quite difficult discipline of study and apprenticeship, and they are expected by their colleagues to adhere to rather rigorous standards in their work before they are considered to be true professionals. These criteria hold for both the so-called "pure" scientists (physicists, biologists, geologists, etc.) and the "applied" scientists (engineers, medical doctors, etc.).

Because of the strong emphasis in the sciences on empiricism, logic, and mathematical rigor, it is not surprising that scientists are expected to be empirical, logical, and quantitative in their personal attitudes and philosophies. They believe only what they can see demonstrated; they insist that a phenomenon is not really understood unless it can be formulated mathematically and measured experimentally.

At least that is the "image" scientists have of themselves! Cool-headed, dispassionate, logical, meticulous, analytical—such adjectives describe scientists, so scientists believe, and so do most other people believe about scientists. There is no place in a scientific mind for such intangibles as faith—especially religious faith in a supernatural Creator and a divinely inspired Book, so they say. "Creation," "God," "miracle"—terms such as these refer to things which cannot be seen or described scientifically and so are unscientific. A man of science cannot also be a man of faith—except, of course, faith in the scientific axiom that one should believe only what one can see or demonstrate.

That is the *image* cultivated by scientists about themselves. The real scientist, however, is commonly a fallible, emotional, credulous, often bigoted and opinionated individual—just like other men and women! Spiritually speaking, he is sinful and proud, just like anybody else. The writer of this book is one such scientist, and he has regularly worked and talked with thousands of other scientists during a career spanning over forty years now, and can testify from abundant personal experience that this is really the way it is. Without in any way belittling the great accomplishments and contributions of scientists and the scientific method, we should never forget that scientists are only ordinary people who have certain types of abilities and have had the opportunity of certain types of training, but who also have the same weaknesses and needs as anyone else.

There is thus absolutely no reason why a scientist should not also be a man of religious faith, like anybody else. There is nothing in science that can ever *prove* that God does not exist and, therefore, no way that science can disprove the possibility of miracles or of true creation. Science cannot either "prove" or "disprove" such things, and so a scientist can decide for himself whether or not he will believe them. The observed facts and data of science can support him in this choice, or otherwise, but they can never compel it. It is completely wrong for people to assume — as they often do — that a true scientist cannot simultaneously be a true man of God, believing in God as Creator and Savior and believing the Bible as God's revelation.

As a matter of fact, many scientists of the past and present have been and are Bible-believing Christians — sinners saved by grace, just like many farmers and clerks and homemakers, people in all walks of life. Nevertheless, the opinion has been widely fostered that "science" has no place for God or faith in the Bible. Particularly damaging has been the pervasive propaganda claiming that science has disproved creation, so that even the origin of all things must be explained in a purely naturalistic, mechanistic context. No scientist can be a creationist, it is said; all true scientists must believe in evolution, it is alleged.

It is because of this false, but widely prevalent, opinion that there has been a growing need to study the religious beliefs of the greatest scientists — those giants of the past who pioneered in the development of science and are the ones who are most responsible for its nature and accomplishments. Were these men skeptics and agnostics? Are their achievements attributable to a mechanistic, atheistic attitude toward the world and its phenomena? Or were they men who believed in God and His sovereignty over nature as its Creator?

In view of the interesting and important nature of such questions, it is surprising to find that very little attention has been paid to them. The only reason why the writer prepared *this* book is because he could find no other similar book already written. Biographies and biographical anthologies abound, but apparently no book has yet been written collecting the biographical testimonies of the great scientists of the past who could be included among the founding fathers of modern science and who were also men who believed the Bible and the basic doctrines of Christianity.

Accordingly, this present book represents only an exploratory survey of this important field of biographical study. Brief biographies are given of 101 of these great men of the past, summarizing both their scientific contributions and their Christian testimonies, insofar as the latter could be determined. Unfortunately, this latter information has not been easy to find, since the standard biographies say little about such things. One must depend mostly on incidental references, comments by their contemporaries, and their own letters and diaries when available.

The writer hopes that Christian biographers and historians, particularly historians of science, will be stimulated by this introductory survey to make a far more thorough study of the subject than this writer has been able to do. A really adequate investigation would require the scholarly study of multitudes of original documents in the great libraries of Europe, as well as America.

Pressures of time and a multitude of other responsibilities have necessarily limited both the scope and depth of *this* book. Nevertheless, it may perhaps at least partially meet a real need at this time, when Christians of all denominations (and those in other religions who still believe in the God of the Bible) want assurance that true science is compatible with Biblical revelation. The knowledge that many of the greatest founders of modern science were believing

Christians will at least refute the common notion that one cannot be both a man of science and a man of God.

Furthermore, there has been no attempt to include in this collection those scientists who were not Christians (orthodox Jews, for example) but who did believe in the one God of creation and in the authority of the Old Testament. Perhaps a chapter on these men can be added in a future edition.

Since this book is intended as a popular-level introduction, with an evangelistic thrust and motivation, rather than as a scholarly monograph, no attempt has been made to include documentation. The sources used are admittedly of varied and uneven quality. In addition to the standard encyclopedias and biographical dictionaries, the writer has consulted mostly his own fairly extensive library and forty-year file collections of journal articles, both scientific and religious. Much more than this needs to be done, of course, and it is hoped that graduate students and other Christian scholars with the necessary time and resources will undertake this kind of research in the near future.

In the meantime, this little book is offered as an introduction and as an encouragement to Christians and honest seekers after truth and life. If readers know of any scientist who should have been included but was overlooked (or if they can show that someone was included who should not have been), they are urged to send that information for future revisions and extensions of the book. The criteria for inclusion are only the following: (1) the scientist was a person of real achievement and significance in the development of science; (2) he was a professing Christian (any denomination) who believed in the divine authority of the Bible; (3) he believed that the universe, life, and man were directly and specially created by the transcendent God of the Bible. Such listings will, of course, incorporate men whose beliefs may be unorthodox in certain ways and can include both Catholics and Protestants, as well as members of small sects. Both "recent creationists" and "progressive creationists" are included, as well as some "theistic evolutionists" (that is, if they believed in the special creation of the universe, the first life forms, and the first human beings). The writer would disagree with the *interpretations* of the Bible advocated by a number of men included in this book, but the purpose here is merely to be guided by their professed belief in its inspiration and authority. Also, no attempt is made to evaluate their personal conduct as professing Christians. Most were undoubtedly "born-again" Christians, but only God knows the true condition of each human heart.

A few men are included (e.g., Agassiz in America, Owen in England, Virchow in Germany) who were not orthodox Christians at all but who were great scientists and were leaders in the scientific fight against evolution. They were hardly "men of God" in the spiritual sense, but were nevertheless key men in the fight for God's foundational truth of special creation at a critical period in the history of science.

Although all these limitations of the book must be kept in mind, it is believed and hoped that it will prove enlightening and encouraging to many readers. *True* science is never at enmity with God, and a true man of science can and should also be a true man of God.

Chapter 1

THE BIBLICAL ORIGINS OF MODERN SCIENCE

One of the most serious fallacies of modern thought is the widespread notion that Biblical Christianity is in conflict with true science and, therefore, that genuine scientists cannot believe the Bible. The scientific method is built on empirical testing of hypotheses, and since creation and other Biblical doctrines cannot be tested in the laboratory, they are considered nonscientific, to be taken strictly on faith. Furthermore, it is commonly believed that the Bible contains many scientific errors. At the very most, it is contended, a scientist may be able to accept the spiritual teachings of the Bible if he wishes, but never its scientific and historical teachings.

Such a charge is tragically wrong, however, and has done untold damage. Thousands of scientists of the past and present have been and are Bible-believing Christians. As a matter of fact, the most discerning historians and philosophers of science have recognized that the very existence of modern science had its origins in a culture at least nominally committed to a Biblical basis, and at a time in history marked by a great return to Biblical faith.

As a matter of fact, authorization for the development of science and technology was specifically commissioned in God's primeval mandate to Adam and Eve (Genesis 1:26-28), and many early scientists, especially in England and America, viewed it in just this way. The study of the world and its processes is really, as Kepler and other great scientists have maintained, "thinking God's thoughts after Him," and should be approached reverently and humbly.

In this book, therefore, are gathered together a number of brief biographical testimonies of important scientists who professed to be Bible-believing Christians. Many of these names are names familiar to every science student, but he may not know that these men also were Christians (this fact is commonly ignored or slighted in present-day scientific literature). This is by no means an exhaustive list, but it should at least put to rest the common misconception that no first-class scientist can be a Bible-believing Christian.

Some of these scientists lived before the rise of modern Darwinism, but they were certainly well aware of evolutionary philosophy (which has been around since antiquity) and of scientific skepticism in general (deism, humanism, atheism, pantheism, and other anti-Biblical philosophies were very real threats to Christian theism

2

long before the modern era). Nevertheless, they were all convinced of the authority of Scripture and the truth of the Christian world view.

Like people in other professions (even preachers), scientists have held a variety of specific religious beliefs. The inclusion of a particular scientist in this collection does not indicate that we would or would not endorse his personal behavior or particular doctrinal or denominational beliefs. Our only criterion has been that, in addition to being a highly qualified scientist, he believed in the inspiration and authority of the Bible, accepted Jesus Christ as the Son of God, and believed in the one true God of the Bible as the Creator of all things. They will also be seen to represent many different fields of science. In other words, there have been leading scientists in every field of science who have studied both the Bible and their own scientific disciplines in depth, and who are firmly convinced the two are fully compatible.

Chapter 2

THE TEST OF EXPERIENCE

For most people the final and unanswerable proof of the truth of the Christian gospel is that it has worked in their own lives. God's promises in His Word have always proved valid when they put them to work.

This is the empirical test, and is the very essence of the scientific method. It should have special significance to all scientists, and even more to engineers and other "applied" scientists and technologists. So-called "pure" scientists and "armchair" scientists may devise and publish speculative theories which may or may not be valid. They must be tested empirically and put to practical use before they really are very meaningful in human life. When the status of a scientific theory is inadequate for a completely rational analysis and design, the engineering scientist must design his structure or system almost entirely on the basis of experimental testing. He cannot base his designs on philosophical speculation or armchair theories. The structure has to be safe; the machine has to function; the process has to work. If available scientific theories are inadequate, which is more often the case than not, empirical tests must be employed for verification purposes.

In like manner, it is perfectly possible to put the claims of Christ and the Bible to empirical test. "I beseech you therefore, brethren, by the mercies of God, that ye present your bodies a living sacrifice, holy, acceptable unto God, which is your reasonable service. And be not conformed to this world: but be ye transformed by the renewing of your mind, that ye may prove what is that good, and acceptable, and perfect, will of God" (Romans 12:1, 2). The promise of God in His Word is: "Believe on the Lord Jesus Christ, and thou shalt be saved, and thy house" (Acts 16:31).

Many scientists and engineers, as well as people from all walks of life, have found such promises empirically true. In fact, no one who has ever acted upon them, in full assurance of an understanding faith, believing in Jesus Christ as Son of God and personal Lord and Savior, has ever found them to fail! "O taste and see that the Lord is good: blessed is the man that trusteth in Him" (Psalm 34:8)

There are many scientists who, in the same way and with the same faith as anyone else, have experienced the miracle of regeneration through personal trust in Christ and His Word. In one sense, however, the testimony of believing scientists may carry special interest and conviction, since they have used their scientific training and analytical abilities on this problem in two distinct empirical ways: (1) they have evaluated the scientific perspective and statements of Scripture in terms of the known data of their own and other scientific fields; (2) they have personally submitted their hearts and minds to Christ in faith, making a direct empirical test of the promises of His Word. In both cases, the results of the test have been firmly positive. The Bible has stood the test of the most searching scientific investigations and has emerged stronger than ever. On the personal level, scientists — even with their ingrained critical skepticism — have proved Christ to be fully satisfying, "able also to save them to the uttermost that come unto God by Him" (Hebrews 7:25).

The arrogant unbelieving skepticism of many modern-day scientists must, therefore, be kept in perspective. The large majority of nonbelieving scientists have never made either of these two tests. Nevertheless they feel they somehow have the authority to speak dogmatically against the Bible and its teachings. The following biographical testimonies of scientist believers should be considered with this contrast in mind.

Even though the doctrinal views of these men cover a wide spectrum of theological opinion and Bible interpretation, they all were firmly committed to belief in a divine Creator and the absolute necessity of intelligent design to explain and organize the sciences they were founding and developing. They were strongly opposed to atheism, pantheism and agnosticism, and would be entirely out of place in the environment of the scientific establishment today. Some might say that they were simply products of their times, forgetting that atheism and evolutionary pantheism were very strong during all these times, with the scientists largely standing solidly against such philosophies. In fact, it was the reviving spirit of Biblical faith associated with the Reformation and the Great Awakening that actually facilitated the rise of modern science, as many historians of science have shown. Many of the early scientists, in fact, were also clergymen.

In any case, the modern idea that science and theistic creationism are incompatible was obviously invalid during the days when the great founders of science were building these sciences!

Chapter 3

THE FOUNDERS OF MODERN SCIENCE

The rise of modern science is generally associated with the Renaissance period, although its roots go back into antiquity. The scientific revolution really got under way with the Protestant Reformation. Prior to that time, scientists almost necessarily had to be nurtured in the educational institutions of the Roman Catholic Church. Within the Church, there was a wide range of beliefs and practices, but many of its most spiritually-minded communicants were also great scientists, men who fully believed in the Bible and in the Deity, atoning death, and bodily resurrection of the Lord Jesus Christ. Coming out of such a background, and across a span of several centuries, it is sometimes difficult to evaluate their personal relationships with the Lord, but there is no reason to doubt the genuineness of their faith.

Leonardo da Vinci (1452 - 1519) is considered by many to be the real founder of modern science, even though he is more widely recognized for his incomparable

Leonardo da Vinci

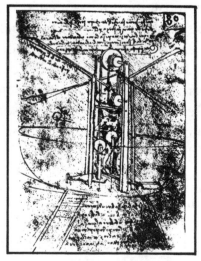

Flying Machine

paintings. He was also a great engineer and architect, designing many of the chief structures and public works of Milan. His scientific notebooks are filled with studies and analyses of problems in dynamics, anatomy, physics, optics, biology, hydraulics, and even aeronautics, all far in advance of his time. He was an experimental scientist long before the formulation of the so-called scientific method.

Leonardo was also, according to all accounts, a man of high moral character, gracious and kind in all dealings. Although his few extant manuscripts deal with art or science, rather than theology, there is no doubt that he was a sincere believer in Christ and the Scriptures, as well as the general faith of the church. If nothing else were available to give this testimony, his great work of art, *The Last Supper*, with its profound insights into the heart of Christ and the disciples, a painting that has blessed and stirred the souls of multitudes over the centuries, would bear witness of his faith.

Johann Kepler (1571 - 1630) is considered to be the founder of physical astronomy. To some extent, he built upon the foundational studies of Copernicus and Tycho Brahe, as well as utilizing the telescope developed by Galileo, but it was he who discovered the laws of planetary motion and who established the discipline of celestial mechanics. He conclusively demonstrated the

Johann Kepler

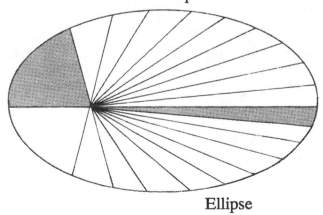

Ellipse

heliocentricity of the solar system and published the first ephemeris tables for tracking star motions, contributing also to eventual development of the calculus.

Kepler was an earnest Christian and studied for two years in a seminary, leaving only with reluctance to enter the study and teaching of astronomy when the Lord opened that door. He was apparently the first scientist to state that, in his astronomical researches, he was merely "thinking God's thoughts after Him," a motto adopted by many believing scientists since his time. His astronomical studies also led him into studies of Biblical chronology, and he believed that the world was created about 7,000 years ago. Kepler wrote in one of his books: "Since we astronomers are priests of the highest God in regard to the book of nature, it befits us to be thoughtful, not of the glory of our minds, but rather, above all else, of the glory of God."

Francis Bacon (1561 - 1626), Lord Chancellor of England, is usually considered to be the man primarily responsible for the formulation and establishment of the so-called "scientific method" in science, stressing experimentation and induction from data rather than philosophical deduction in the tradition of Aristotle. Bacon's writings are also credited with leading to the founding of the Royal Society of London.

Francis Bacon

Sir Francis was a devout believer in the Bible. He wrote: "There are two books laid before us to study, to prevent our falling into error; first, the volume of the Scriptures, which reveal the will of God; then the volume of the Creatures, which express His power."

Blaise Pascal (1623 - 1662) was one of the greatest early philosophers and mathematicians and is considered the father of the science of hydrostatics and one of the founders of hydrodynamics. In mathematics, he laid the foundation for the modern treatment of conic sections, as well as differential calculus and the mathematical theory of probability. His other scientific and mathematical contributions were legion, including the development of the barometer.

He is equally famous, however, for his religious contributions, his best-known work being his *Pensees*. He was a deeply spiritual man, a leader of the sect known as the Jansenists, a Calvinistic quasi-Protestant group within the Catholic Church. To him is attributed the famous Wager of Pascal, paraphrased as follows: "How can anyone lose who chooses to become a Christian? If, when he dies, there turns out to be no God and his faith was in vain, he has lost nothing — in fact, he has been happier in life than his nonbelieving friends, If, however, there is a God and a heaven and hell, then he has gained heaven and his skeptical friends will have lost everything in hell!"

Robert Boyle (1627 - 1691), one of the founders of the Royal Society of London, is generally credited with being the father of modern chemistry, as distinct from the alchemy of the middle ages. His name is associated with the basic law which he discovered relating gas pressures to temperature and volume, the fundamental principle of gas dynamics. His contributions in both physics and chemistry are very great in number, and he was considered in his time to be probably the greatest physical scientist of his generation.

Yet he was also a humble, witnessing Christian and a diligent student of the Bible. He was profoundly interested in missions and devoted much of his own money to Bible translation work and the propagation of the gospel. He was strong in apologetics, founding via his will the "Boyle lectures" for proving the Christian religion.

John Ray (1627 - 1705), has been called the father of English natural history. He made extensive collections and catalogs of English flora in particular. Along with Boyle, he was one the founding members of the Royal Society. He was the greatest authority of his day in both botany and zoology.

Robert Boyle

Ray was also a strong Christian and creationist, writing a number of books on natural theology, chief of which was *The Wisdom of God Manifested in the Works of the Creation*. God's works of creation, he said, were "the works created by God at first, and by Him conserved to this day in the same state and condition in which they were first made." Much of his efforts were directed toward opposing the deistic evolutionists of his day, especially Descartes (1596 - 1650) and his followers on the Continent.

Nicolaus Steno (1631 - 1686) , also known as Nils Stennsen, was born in Denmark, but spent much of his life in Italy. In this section we have noted the remarkable fact that the "founding fathers" of many important branches of science were earnest Christian believers. This is even true of that branch of science which, in our day, has been used as a chief bulwark of evolutionism, namely the science of stratigraphy. Steno, with his extensive field studies, developed the principles of stratigraphical interpretation which are still considered basic today.

However, he also interpreted the strata – unlike modern evolutionary stratigraphers – in the manner of flood geologists, attributing their formation in large measure to the Great Flood. The fossils did not represent "figured stones," as many geologists of the time believed, but remains of actual plants and animals living at the time of the Flood. Steno eventually took up orders and a religious vocation, writing numerous theological works and becoming a bishop.

Thomas Burnet (1635 - 1715) was an English clergyman and also one of the first geologists, author of a very influential work entitled *Sacred Theory of the Earth*. In this work, he took the Scriptural account of creation and the flood as providing the basic framework of interpretation for earth history, showing it to be confirmed by known facts of physics and geology.

Athanasius Kircher (1601 - 1680) was a learned Jesuit who published a treatise on Noah's Ark and the effect of the flood on the earth's land surfaces. He made a number of scientific studies which anticipated later breakthroughs, including the partial deciphering of Egyptian hieroglyphics and the germ theory of disease. He invented a magic lantern, an aeolian harp and other devices.

John Wilkins (1614 - 1672), like many in his day, was both a clergyman and a scientist, defending both the Biblical warrant for scientific study and the scientific evidence supporting theism and Christianity. He was a leading organizing spirit of the growing scientific movement, with a number of his proteges soon forming the

Royal Society. Although he tended to argue for keeping the spheres of scientific and religious authority distinct, he did provide a number of scientific arguments supporting Scripture, from evidence in nature for God to the adequate size of Noah's ark to accommodate all the animals.

Walter Charleton (1619-1707) was an active early member of the Royal Society and also served as President of the Royal College of Physicians. In his religious writings he sought diligently to find divine purpose in every act of nature. He defended the Biblical miracles, as well as creation and the flood.

Sir William Petty (1623 - 1687) was one of the first members of the Royal Society and an active defender of the faith. He helped to found the science of statistics and the modern study of economics. He practiced medicine successfully and served many years as a public official. He wrote many papers showing evidence of God's design in nature.

Isaac Barrow (1630 - 1677) was professor of mathematics at Cambridge, even teaching math to Isaac Newton and thus laying the foundations for Newton's discovery of calculus. However, he was a strong and orthodox Christian who finally resigned to devote his life to preaching God's Word. More than most preachers of his age, his ministry was fully Christ-centered, not only in doctrine but in life.

Increase Mather (1639 - 1723) is best known as a clergyman and leading theologian in colonial New England, the father of Cotton Mather. He was also an avid avocational astronomer and promoter of science in the colonies. He was the primary founder of the Philosophical Society and one of the first presidents of Harvard, when that school was still sound and zealous in the Christian faith. He diligently studied comets and wrote a number of monographs on them.

Nehemiah Grew (1641 - 1712) was both a medical doctor and a botanist, doing important research and writing on plant anatomy. He also wrote extensively on the evidence of unique creative design in both plants and animals. An orthodox Protestant, he was one of the first members of the Royal Society, strongly defending Biblical truth and authority.

Many other prominent scientists of the 16th and 17th centuries, while perhaps not as overtly Christian as those listed above, were at least intellectually committed to the

Scriptures and to Christ, as well as to a belief in special creation. Even though **Galileo (1564 - 1642)**, for example, was officially censured for his heliocentric teachings by the Church, he himself believed the Bible and that it supported his views. **Robert Hooke (1635 - 1703)**, brilliant physicist and geologist, **William Harvey (1578 - 1657)**, who discovered the circulation of the blood, **Christian Huygens (1629 - 1695)**, **Tycho Brahe (1545 - 1601)** and **Nicholas Copernicus (1473 - 1543)** are further examples of the numerous scientists of this period who were at least theistic creationists.

Hooke's Scope

Chapter 4

THE AGE OF NEWTON

Most scholars who have studied the question have judged Sir Isaac Newton to have been the greatest scientist who ever lived. He, built on the foundation laid by others, but his tremendous discoveries provided the solid framework within which the great scientific and industrial revolutions of the 18th century could develop.

Isaac Newton (1642 - 1727) is famous for, among other things, his discovery of the law of universal gravitation, the formulation of the three laws of motion which make possible the discipline of dynamics and all its subdivisions, and his development of the calculus into a comprehensive branch of mathematics, now a basic tool in every science. He anticipated the great law of energy conservation, developed the particle theory of light propagation, and as an astronomer constructed the first reflecting telescope.

This man of gigantic intellect was also a genuine believer in Christ as his Savior and in the Bible as God's Word. He wrote many books on Biblical subjects, especially

Isaac Newton

Newton & Astronomy

prophecy. This was not a senile aberration, as some have alleged, as he was a committed believer from his youth. He even wrote a book defending the Ussher Chronology against those who would try to push back the date of creation. He wrote strong papers refuting atheism and defending creation and the Bible. He believed that the worldwide Flood of the Bible accounted for most of the geological phenomena, and he believed in the literal six-day creation record. Finally, he said: "We account the Scriptures of God to be the most sublime philosophy. I find more sure marks of authenticity in the Bible than in any profane history whatsoever."

William Whiston (1667 - 1752) was the successor to Sir Isaac Newton at Cambridge University (1703). He had dedicated to Sir Isaac his book *A New Theory of the Earth* which, like that of Thomas Burnet, was a harmony of the Biblical record of creation and the flood with the growing data of physics and geology. Newton himself responded very favorably to both works. Although both seemed to make perhaps too much of an attempt to devise strictly naturalistic explanations for the phenomena involved, they did accept the Biblical accounts as fully historical, with their implication of a recent creation and flood geology.

John Woodward (1665 - 1728) was a close friend of Newton's and ranks with Steno as one of the true founding fathers of the science of geology. An avid collector of fossils, one of Woodward's valuable contributions was the establishment of a great paleontological museum at Cambridge and the Woodwardian Professorship of Geology there. He had been Professor of Medicine at Gresham College in London. He held a high regard for the Bible, as well as a thorough field knowledge of geology. His book *Essay Towards a Natural History of the Earth* was both more soundly Biblical and more scientific geologically than its predecessors. Its treatment of flood geology is still very valuable.

Carolus Linnaeus (1707 - 1778) is widely regarded as the father of biological taxonomy. The standard classification system of plants and animals still used today is known as the Linnaean system. He was a man of great piety and respect for the Scriptures. One of his main goals in systematizing the tremendous varieties of living creatures was to attempt to delineate the original Genesis "kinds." He attempted, in fact, to equate his "species" category with the "kind," believing that variation could occur within the kind, but not from one kind to another kind. Thus he believed in the "fixity of species," even

Carolus Linneaus

though he realized that he could well make mistakes in identifying any given original kind.

Jonathan Edwards (1703 - 1758) is not generally known as a scientist, but as a theologian and college president, a leader of American thought in the colonies. Nevertheless, while still in his teens, Edwards exhibited deep understanding and original insights into physics, meteorology, and astronomy, far in advance of his time. He continued to exhibit an aptitude in science throughout a busy career in missionary, pastoral, and educational work. He could almost certainly have become an outstanding man of science during a critical epoch in the development of science, but the Lord had other plans for him, and he was destined to play a key role in the colonies' Great Awakening and to help prepare them for the unique spiritual ministry they would one day have in world history.

William Herschel (1738 - 1822) has long been recognized as both an outstanding Christian and an outstanding astronomer. In astronomy he made many great discoveries, perhaps the most notable being the recognition of double stars and the discovery of Uranus. He constructed the greatest reflecting telescopes of his day and cataloged and studied the nebulae and galaxies as never before.

As a Christian, Sir William was said by his biographer to be "a great, simple, good old man," noted for his kindness and his sublime conception of the universe as a marvelous witness to the handiwork of God. it was Herschel who said: "The undevout astronomer must be mad."

John Harris (1666 - 1719) was an early English mathematician, as well as a clergyman. He was editor of *The Dictionary of Arts and Sciences* in 1704, considered to be the first real encyclopedia in the English language. He was an early member and vice president of the Royal Society. He also was an active Christian apologist, giving the Boyle lectures in 1698 under the title: "Atheistical Objections Against the Being of God and His Attributes, Fairly Considered and Fully Refuted."

Gottfried Wilhelm Leibnitz (1646 - 1716) was one of the world's most gifted mathematicians and philosophers. A contemporary of Sir Isaac Newton, he was co-discoverer with Newton of calculus, also anticipating the fundamental scientific principle of energy conservation. He introduced the binary notational system and anticipated the Boolean system of logic. He made many other scientific and mathematical contributions, but is perhaps best known for his "theodicy," a philosophical and theological study attempting to prove that this is the best of all possible worlds. Although somewhat heterodox in doctrine, he firmly believed in God and even wrote a defense of the doctrine of the Trinity. He spent much effort (unsuccessfully) trying to define theological common ground for the reunion of the Catholic and Protestant churches and also, later, for the reunion of the Lutheran and Reformed Churches.

John Flamsteed (1646 - 1719) was the founder of the famous Greenwich observatory and the first Astronomer Royal of England. He produced the first great star map of the telescopic age, after innumerable observations. The meridians of the world are, as a result, referenced to 0° longitude through his observatory. He was also a faithful clergyman, very devout in his life and preaching.

William Derham (1657 - 1735) was one of the Boyle lecturers, his treatise (*Physico-Theology*) being a strong exposition of purposive design in nature by the God of the Bible. He was probably the first writer to argue for the study of science as a stewardship from God, very much in the vein of modern ecology. In a sense, he could be considered the father of ecology.

Cotton Mather (1662 - 1727) was, like his father, a clergyman, theologian and president of Harvard. He also studied medicine and was probably the first American to publish original contributions in science, with many publications in the *Transactions of the Royal Society*. Among other things, he studied "animalcules" as a cause of smallpox, and was effective in routing it from the colonies.

John Hutchinson (1674 - 1737) was both a Hebrew scholar and an early student of paleontology, following his friend and colleague John Woodward. As Steward to the Duke of Somerset, he developed a strong system of natural philosophy fully consistent with orthodox Christianity. Like Woodward, he strongly defended the Biblical flood as the cause of all major geological landforms.

Gustavus Brander (1720 - 1787) was an English naturalist and paleontologist, whose abundant fossil collections are now in the British Museum. He wrote in defense of flood geology against the then-growing interest in long geological ages and uniformity. He was a Fellow of the Royal Society and a Trustee of the British Museum.

Jean Deluc (1727 - 1817) was a Swiss naturalist and physicist who studied geology and actually coined the word "geology." He was strongly committed to the Genesis record of creation and the worldwide flood. He and his father developed the modern mercury thermometer and the hygrometer. He wrote books on both geology and meteorology and ardently opposed Buffon's evolutionary theories.

Richard Kirwan (1733 - 1812) was an Irish chemist and mineralogist, president of the Royal Irish Academy for 23 years, and author of the first systematic treatise on mineralogy, also making many contributions to chemistry. He also advocated flood geology and vigorously opposed the increasingly influential uniformitarian theories of James Hutton, the predecessor of Sir Charles Lyell.

James Parkinson (1755 - 1824) was an English physician who made a number of significant medical discoveries. These included recognition of the nature and danger of a perforated appendix, and first describing the condition known ever since as "Parkinson's disease." He was also an ardent amateur geologist, apparently the first to recognize the plant origin of coal. He also wrote extensively on the Biblical flood and its geological effects, especially in the formation of coal and oil.

Although there were other notable Christian scientists of the 18th century, the tide of unbelief was rising. Especially on the Continent, such men as Spinoza, Kant, Descartes, LaPlace, and others were turning many intellectuals to pantheism, or deism, or atheism. The study of geology was beginning to lead people back to the long-age concepts of ancient pagan philosophies. Similarly, evolutionism, though long out of fashion among scientists, had been advocated by various liberal theologians and social philosophers, and it was beginning also to creep back into the scientific literature. Erasmus Darwin (1731 - 1802), for example, published books on evolution before his more famous grandson, Charles, was born. So did Comte de Buffon (1707 - 1788). The prolific evolutionist writer, Jean Baptiste Lamarck (1744 - 1829) began to have a profound effect at the close of the century.

In the 19th century, however, even though evolutionism and then atheism would eventually come to dominate the scientific community, God was still raising up great men of science to witness for Him, even under such circumstances.

Chapter 5

JUST BEFORE DARWIN

In the six decades of the 19th century, before the appearance of Darwin's *Origin of Species*, the climate of the western world was increasingly one of religious skepticism. The industrial revolution had fostered a climate of evolutionary optimism; at the same time its excesses were also creating a spirit of revolution. Nevertheless, faith in God and the Bible were still strong, especially in America. Scientists for the most part maintained at least nominal allegiance to the Scriptures, but there was a strong undercurrent of doubt and desire to cast off these shackles. When Darwin proposed his theory of natural selection, it was like a dam breaking, and in only a few short years practically the entire scientific world seemed to have capitulated to unbelief. Nevertheless, even in this period there were many notable men of science who maintained strong and vital Christian testimonies.

Michael Faraday (1791 - 1867)is universally acknowledged as one of the greatest physicists of all time. He was especially gifted in scientific experimentation,

Michael Faraday

particularly in developing the new sciences of electricity and magnetism. He discovered electromagnetic induction and introduced the concept of magnetic lines of force. He invented the generator and made many other key discoveries and inventions. Two basic units, one in electrolysis, one in electrostatics, are named in his honor. He also made many key contributions in the field of chemistry.

Yet this great man was one of the most humble and sincere Christians one could ever find. His family was desperately poor, but deeply spiritual, members of the Sandemanian sect, a small fundamentalist church whose teaching included emphasis on God's creation as purposeful and harmonious, designed for man's well-being. He had an abiding faith in the Bible and in prayer. Unlike Newton, however, he made little attempt to "harmonize" his science with his Biblical faith, supremely confident that the two were both based on divine truth and were necessarily in agreement. He was very regular and faithful in the various ministries of his church, both public and personal. He fully believed in the official doctrine of his church, which said: "The Bible, and it alone, with nothing added to it nor taken away from it by man, is the sole and sufficient guide for each individual, at all times and in all circumstances . . . Faith in the divinity and work of Christ is the gift of God, and the evidence of this faith is obedience to the commandment of Christ."

Humphrey Davy (1778 - 1829) was one of the great chemists of this period, the man under whom Faraday served as apprentice and who inspired Faraday to devote his life to science. Sir Humphrey was the first to isolate many important chemical elements, to develop the motion theory of heat, to invent the safety lamp, and to demonstrate that diamond is carbon, along with many other vital contributions. Like his young friend, Faraday, he was a Bible-believing Christian, highly altruistic and generous, though not as spiritually minded and patient as was Faraday. He was also a poet and, for a while, something of a Christian mystic. In his declining years, however, he returned to Biblical Christianity and found peace therein.

Georges Cuvier (1769 - 1832) was one of the greatest anatomists and paleontologists; in fact, he is considered to be the founder of the science of comparative anatomy and one of the chief architects of paleontology as a separate scientific discipline. He was the chief advocate of the theory of multiple catastrophism, believing the Flood to be the last in a series of global castastrophes in earth history. He was a firm creationist, even participating in important creation/evolution debates.

Timothy Dwight (1752 - 1817) was not a scientist in the strict sense, but rather a preacher and educator. However, he was tremendously powerful in an apologetics ministry, including the firm relating of science to Scripture. Among his writings are included excellent expositions of flood geology. As president of Yale, he was almost solely responsible for converting the student body and faculty of that key institution from profligate unbelief and revolutionism to a soundly Biblical evangelistic and missionary commitment, a transformation accomplished mainly through a lengthy series of closely-reasoned chapel messages on scientific Christian apologetics. He is said to have had influence on the character of the infant nation of America second only to that of George Washington.

Benjamin Silliman (1779 - 1864) was one Yale faculty member profoundly influenced by President Dwight. He wrote: "It would delight your heart to see how the trophies of the cross are multiplied in this institution. Yale College is a little temple: prayer and praise seem to be the delight of the greater part of the students." Silliman graduated from Yale the year following Dwight's arrival and then joined the faculty five years later, becoming

America's outstanding mineralogist and geologist at the time. With Dwight's encouragement, he founded what became the Sheffield Scientific School at Yale, as well as the influential *American Journal of Science*, still one of the world's leading geological journals. He was the first president of the Association of American Geologists and a charter member of the National Academy of Sciences.

Charles Bell (1774 - 1842) was one of the greatest anatomists and surgeons. Author of many volumes, he was Professor of Comparative Anatomy at the Royal College of Surgeons in England. His best known work, as far as the general public was concerned, was his Bridgewater Treatise on *The Hand; Its Mechanism and Vital Endowments, and Evincing Design, and Illustrating the Power, Wisdom, and Goodness of God.* His non-Christian but sympathetic biographer says: "Much of Bell's writing reflects his deeply religious nature, and there can be little doubt that for him the story of Creation was simply revealed truth."

William Buckland (1784 - 1856) was one of the key British geologists in the transition period from Biblical catastrophism to uniformitarianism. As a priest in the Church of England, eventually Dean of Westminster, he was a Bible-believing Christian. In addition, being trained in the sciences of geology and mineralogy, he became a professor in these disciplines at Oxford. He was a strong creationist and wrote a number of books showing the evidences of design found in these two sciences. Moreover, he was a follower of Cuvier's multiple catastrophism and later an advocate of Agassiz' glacial geology, even though he did accept the geologic significance of the worldwide Flood.

Charles Babbage (1792 - 1871) was a fascinating scientist, in many respects far ahead of his time. Primarily a mathematician, he worked on what we now would denote "operations research." He developed the first actuarial tables, invented the first speedometer, and the first skeleton keys, as well as the first ophthalmoscope and the first locomotive "cowcatcher." His most important work, however, was in the development of the first true computers, including the use of punched-card directions and information storage and retrieval systems.

As a Christian, he wrote the ninth and last of the Bridgewater Treatises, a remarkable apologetic including a mathematical analysis of the Biblical miracles.

David Brewster (1781 - 1868) founded the science of optical mineralogy, describing light polarization and inventing the kaleidoscope. He also made notable studies in astronomy, and received many scientific prizes and honors. He was one of the founders of the British Association for Advancement of Science, later serving as its president. One paper he published in the Association's journal described a large nail found embedded in a large stone taken from a quarry. This discovery was, of course, ignored by the scientific world, which had recently become enamored of the geological ages.

As Darwinism came on the scene, Brewster was one of its chief opponents in the scientific world for both scientific and Biblical reasons. He had studied for the ministry and combined his scientific research with preaching the Word. The Lord became much more personally real to him, however, after the death of his wife, when he experienced a true conversion and regeneration.

John Herschel (1792 - 1871) was the son of Sir William Herschel and, like his father, was both an outstanding astronomer and devout Christian. He discovered over 500 new nebulae and performed the prodigious task of cataloging the stars and nebulae of both northern and southern hemispheres. Concerning the Bible, he said: "All human discoveries seem to be made only for the purpose of confirming more and more strongly the truths come from on high and contained in the sacred writings."

John Dalton (1766 - 1844) was born in a Quaker family and was a practicing Quaker all his life, during a time when Quakers were all known as orthodox and pious Bible-believing Christians. Throughout his life, he was known as a godly man, of very simple tastes and life-style. In science, he is best recognized today as the father of modern atomic theory, which revolutionized the study of chemistry. His first love, however was meteorology, and he formulated the well-known gas law of partial pressures. He was also the first to recognize and describe the phenomenon of color-blindness, a condition also known ever since as Daltonism.

Dalton was one of the founders of the British Association for Advancement of Science, in 1831. One year later he was awarded a doctorate by Oxford University.

William Kirby (1759 - 1850) was an English clergyman and entomologist. He wrote many devotional and many scientific works, including a four-volume *Introduction to Entomology*. He is best known, however, for his authorship of two of the famous Bridgewater Treatises, Volumes X and XI, with the title: *On the Power and Wisdom of God and His Goodness as Manifested in the Creation of Animals*, with a shorter subtitle: *On the History, Habits and Instincts of Animals*. He also wrote extensively on flood geology, even including a very relevant exposition of II Peter 3:3-7.

Jedidiah Morse (1761 - 1826) was a godly Congregational minister and father of Samuel F. B. Morse, inventor of the telegraph. He was also the leading geographer of America during his lifetime. He wrote the first American textbook of geography, almost universally used in the schools of the day and going through 25 editions, many of them after his death. He was a strong advocate of flood geology and the literal-day Mosaic chronology of earth history. His geography textbook included a scholarly discussion of the preservation of Earth's animals in Noah's Ark and their subsequent geographical distribution around the earth by means of ancient land bridges.

Benjamin Barton (1766 - 1815) was a prominent American physician, botanist and zoologist, a professor at the University of Pennsylvania. He wrote the first American textbook on botany, as well as the natural history of the Lewis and Clark expedition. As a Christian, he was vitally interested in ethnology and the origin of the different tribes and nations. In his writings he defended the Biblical doctrine of the unity of the human race and their dispersion from Ararat. He also believed in recent creation as the Bible describes.

Samuel Miller (1770 - 1840) was a Presbyterian minister who wrote a definitive and very influential history of the scientific advances in the eighteenth century, a two-volume work entitled *Brief Retrospect of the Eighteenth Century.* Throughout his comprehensive treatise, whether dealing with the scientific studies of Christians or infidels, he stressed the harmony of true science with the Christian faith and Biblical inspiration, including a strong defense of flood geology and a recent creation.

John Kidd, M.D. (1775 - 1851) was Professor of Chemistry at Oxford during most of his career, and made many significant contributions in this field. He pioneered in the use of coal as a source of chemicals, his work eventually providing the foundation for the development of synthetics. As a well-respected Christian, he was chosen to present one of the Bridgewater Treatises, entitled *The Adaptation of Nature to the Physical Condition of Man.*

Peter Mark Roget (1779 - 1869) was an English physician and physiologist, one of the founders of the University of London and the Medical School at

Manchester. He is best known, however, for the famous *Roget's Thesaurus*, used by countless writers for five generations. He also authored one of the famous Bridgewater Treatises, *Animal and Vegetable Physiology Considered with Reference to Natural Theology*.

Thomas Chalmers (1780 - 1847) was a leader in the Church of Scotland and professor of theology in the University of Edinburgh. He authored the first two Bridgewater Treatises, published in two volumes under the title *The Adaptation of External Nature to the Moral and Intellectual Constitution of Man*. He wrote extensively on both the natural and social sciences, as well as theology, and was chiefly responsible for the popularization of the "gap theory" as a supposed defense of the Genesis record against the uniformitarian geologists.

William Prout (1785 - 1850) authored one of the Bridgewater Treatises: *Chemistry, Meteorology, and the Function of Digestion, Considered with Reference to Natural Theology*. As a chemist and physiologist, he was an early leader in the sciences of nutrition and digestion, and was the first to identify basic foodstuffs as fats, proteins and carbohydrates. He is best known, however, for recognizing that the atomic weights of elements could be identified as a series of relative whole numbers.

Samuel F. B. Morse (1791 - 1872) is justly famous for his invention of the telegraph, one of the most important milestones in human history. The first message sent (in 1844) over the wire, "What hath God wrought!" (Numbers 23:23) was indicative of Morse's whole life and purpose, desiring to honor the Lord in all things.

Morse was another great man who had been profoundly influenced by Timothy Dwight at Yale, where he graduated in 1810. In addition to his inventive genius, Morse was an outstanding artist, serving for 20 years as the founder and first president of the National Academy of Design. In 1831 he was appointed Professor of Sculpture and Painting at New York University, the first chair of fine arts in America. He also built the first camera in America and made the world's first photographic portrait. Today he is ranked among the greatest portrait artists of all time.

Just four years before he died, Morse wrote: "The nearer I approach to the end of my pilgrimage, the clearer is the evidence of the divine origin of the Bible, the grandeur and sublimity of God's remedy for fallen man are more appreciated, and the future is illumined with hope and joy."

Samuel F. B. Morse

Joseph Henry (1797 - 1878) was a great American physicist and professor at Princeton University. He discovered the principle of self-induction (the standard unit for which is named after him) and invented the electromagnetic motor and the galvanometer. He was the first Secretary and Director of the Smithsonian Institution, one of the charter members of the National Academy of Sciences, and a founder and early president of the American Association for the Advancement of Science. He was also a devout Christian, in all his experimentation making it a regular practice to stop, to worship God, and then to pray for divine guidance at every important juncture of the experiment.

Matthew Maury (1806 - 1873), known as "the Pathfinder of the Seas" was, to all intents and purposes, the founder of the modern sciences of hydrography and oceanography. On his tombstone at the U.S. Naval Academy is inscribed the eighth Psalm, especially verse 8: "...whatsoever passeth through the paths of the seas." He believed if God said there were *paths* in the seas, it should be possible to find them, and he dedicated his life to doing just that. Most of his career was spent with the U.S. Navy, charting the winds and currents of the Atlantic, with his latter years spent as Professor of Meteorology at Virginia Military Institute.

Matthew Maury

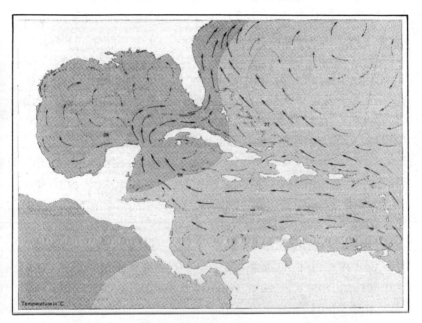

Ocean Currents

James Simpson (1811 - 1870) was born in Scotland and was practically nurtured on the Bible. Considered by the medical profession as one of the chief founders of gynecology, he was Professor of Obstetric Medicine at Edinburgh University. However, he is best known as the discoverer of chloroform in 1847, helping to lay the foundation of modern anesthesiology. He is said to have derived the motivation for the research leading to this discovery by the record of Adam's "deep sleep" in Genesis, when Eve was formed. His greatest discovery, however, according to his own testimony, was: "That I have a Saviour!" A gospel tract written by Sir James, concludes with these words: "But again I looked and saw Jesus, my substitute, scourged in my stead and dying on the cross for me. I looked and cried and was forgiven. And it seems to be my duty to tell you of that Saviour, to see if you will not also look and live. 'He was wounded for our transgressions, . . . and with His stripes we are healed' (Isaiah 53:5,6)."

James Joule (1818 - 1889) conducted numerous studies on heat flow and received many honors. No doubt his greatest discovery (made in 1840), however, was the value of the constant known as the "mechanical equivalent of heat," making possible the quantitative conversion of heat energy into mechanical energy, and vice versa. This conversion factor led to the formulation of the law of conservation of energy, the most basic and universal of all scientific laws. It is surely appropriate that the privilege of making such a vital discovery was given by God to a man of sincere Christian faith. Since the energy conservation principle is the first law of thermodynamics, Joule can rightly be considered the chief founder of thermodynamics as a scientific discipline.

Adam Sedgwick (1785 - 1873) was one of England's leading 19th century geologists, long-time professor of geology at Cambridge, especially famous for identifying and naming the major rock systems known as Cambrian and Devonian. He was also a clergyman and Bible-believing Christian, even though his studies eventually contributed to the development of the system of geological ages. Although he was a friend of Charles Darwin, he always opposed his evolutionary ideas, prophesying that their result would be devastatingly harmful to the world.

William Whewell (1794 - 1866) served at Cambridge University as an Anglican clergyman almost all his life. As a scientist he authored one of the Bridgewater Treatises: *Astronomy and General Physics Considered with*

Reference to Natural Theology. His scientific interests were wide ranging. He is credited with naming the Eocene, Miocene and Pliocene geological epochs, as well as coining the scientific terms *anode, cathode,* and *ion.* In fact, he was even the inventor of the terms *scientist* and *physicist,* as well as the term *catastrophism* in geology, which he defended against uniformitarianism. He made important contributions to the study of tides, and invented the anemometer.

Henry Rogers (1808 - 1866) was an American geologist well known for his detailed studies of the geology of the Appalachians and also of the coal fields of America and Great Britain. For the last nine years of his life, he was professor of natural history and philosophy at the University of Glasgow. He believed in the Biblical flood as of great geological significance and was one of the signers of the 1865 scientists' "Declaration" affirming the scientific integrity of Scripture (see p. 75).

During this period, there were also a rapidly increasing number of unbelieving scientists, as well as unbelievers in other fields of intellectual endeavor. The above scientific men of faith were certainly not living in a vacuum, but in an arena, and they had to "contend for the faith," even as we do today.

Chapter 6

JUST AFTER DARWIN

The publication of Charles Darwin's *Origin of Species* was a watershed of history. Within ten years, practically the whole intellectual world had accepted evolution, and Darwin has ever since been considered one of the most important scientists who ever lived. Even most theologians hastened to jump on the evolutionary bandwagon, along with all the social scientists and innumerable others. This development was soon followed by a tidal wave of humanism, socialism, communism, fascism, laissez-faire capitalism, and other philosophies based on evolution.

Nevertheless, even in this difficult intellectual environment, there were still many outstanding men of science who believed the Bible and maintained a strong Christian testimony. Some of these sincerely believed they could harmonize the new evolutionary concepts with the Bible and Christian doctrine, but many continued also to believe in a special creation.

Louis Agassiz (1807 - 1873) was a great Christian paleontologist and is recognized as the father of glacial geology and the science of glaciology. His studies of fishes, both living and fossil, were definitive, and have never been equaled. He was also a great teacher, both in Europe and America, where his Harvard classes in natural history were said to have produced all the notable teachers of that subject in America during the last half of the 19th century. The great Museum of Comparative Zoology at Harvard was established by him and is named in his honor. While still in Switzerland, his studies of Alpine glaciers led him to the concept of the Pleistocene Ice Age, which most creationists believe to be the only real epoch in the so-called "Geologic Ages."

Agassiz was the son of a preacher and descended from a long line of Huguenot clergymen. He profoundly believed in God and His special creation of every kind of organism. Probably no man was more intimately acquainted with a greater variety of kinds of animals, living and extinct, and it is significant that he was an inveterate opponent of evolutionism to the very end of his life. On the other hand, he seldom attended church, and many have questioned whether he was a Christian in the Biblical sense.

James Dana (1813 - 1895) was an American geologist, successor at Yale to Professor Silliman (whose daughter he married) and author of many influential books on geology and mineralogy. He was an early president of both the Geological Society of America and the American Association for the Advancement of Science. Although he became partly convinced of evolutionism, he continued to believe in Biblical Christianity. He gave this testimony: "The grand old Book of God still stands; and this old earth, the more its leaves are turned over and pondered, the more it will sustain and illustrate the sacred Word."

John William Dawson (1820 - 1899) was the greatest of the early Canadian geologists, contributing significantly to the elucidation of the geology of Canada. He was the first president of the Royal Society of Canada and also was elected president of the American Association for Advancement of Science. He was knighted in 1884. Sir William was a devout Christian and anti-evolutionist, even though he accepted the long-age concept of geology. He not only wrote many geological papers and books, but also a number of Biblical and creationist works.

George Stokes (1819 - 1903) was a great British physicist and mathematician, making major contributions in many fields. One of the most significant of his studies was the development of the science of real fluids, laying the foundation of the modern engineering science of fluid mechanics. He held the chair at Cambridge University once occupied by Isaac Newton. Sir George was a godly Christian gentleman, especially known for his humility. He wrote a book on *Natural Theology* and frequently testified of his faith, even when speaking before learned scientific societies. He specifically wrote emphasizing his belief in the deity and bodily resurrection of Jesus Christ.

Charles Piazzi Smyth (1819 - 1900) was Astronomer Royal for Scotland and Professor of Astronomy at the University of Edinburgh. He also made extensive studies at the Great Pyramid in Egypt and became a founder and leader of the cult of pyramidology and Anglo-Israelism. He also published many significant studies on astronomy and meteorology. Though his commitment to the British-Israel concept may have been unfortunate, he did believe the Bible and sought diligently to apply its teaching to his scientific studies.

Rudolph Virchow (1821 - 1902) is included here because of his strong opposition to the evolutionary teachings of Darwin and Haeckel, as well as his strong social conscience. He opposed the racist teachings of Nietzsche and Bismarck and was responsible for major hospital reforms and public health measures. He was active in anthropological and archeological research and believed these supported the Biblical view of history. However, his main scientific contributions were in the field of medicine. He is considered the father of modern pathology and the study of cellular diseases. He was the first to describe leukemia and made many other important contributions. He also entered actively into politics and fought vigorously against allowing evolutionist teachings in the schools of Germany. On the other hand, he was considered a radical and a materialist by many, and the real nature of his religious convictions is unknown.

Philip H. Gosse (1810 - 1888) was a British ornithologist and author of numerous books on zoology. He was made a fellow of the Royal Society in 1865. As a Christian, he was an active member of the Plymouth Brethren sect. He is best known today for his book *Omphalos: An Attempt to Untie the Geological Knot*, in which he put forth the theory of creation of apparent age in the geological record, carrying it to the extreme of the creation of actual fossils and strata looking as though they had been deposited by normal sedimentation. His theory is often ridiculed today, but both his Biblical faith and scientific knowledge were genuine and recognized.

Gregory Mendel (1822 - 1884) may seem out of place in this list at first, since we know little of his personal beliefs. However, he chose a monastic calling at a time when this certainly included belief in the basic doctrines of Christianity. He was a creationist and rejected Darwin's evolutionary ideas, although he was quite familiar with them.

His experiments with peas, carefully controlled and mathematically analyzed, provided the basis for the understanding of heredity, so that Mendel is rightly considered the father of genetics. It is remarkable that his studies clearly established the basic stability of the created kinds of plants and animals, while evolutionists for many decades have labored to incorporate them somehow into the framework of Darwinism.

Louis Pasteur (1822 - 1895) is one of the greatest names in the history of science and medicine, chiefly because of his establishment of the germ theory of disease and his conclusive demolition of the then-prevalent evolutionary concept of spontaneous generation. He was a physicist and chemist by training and practice and made significant contributions in these fields. He was the first to explain the organic basis and control of fermentation, and as his research led him more and more into bacteriology, he isolated a number of disease-producing organisms and developed vaccines to combat them – notably the dread diseases of rabies, diphtheria, anthrax, and others – as well as the processes of pasteurization and sterilization. He

Louis Pasteur

undoubtedly made the greatest contribution of any one man to the saving of human lives, and most scientists today would say he was the greatest biologist of all time.

Yet, in his lifetime, he was the object of intense opposition by almost the entire biological establishment, because of his own opposition to spontaneous generation and to Darwinism. It was only his persistence and sound experimental and analytical procedures that finally compelled most biological and medical scientists to give up their ideas of the naturalistic origin of life and their treatment of disease as based on this notion. Pasteur was a strongly religious man, and ever more so as he grew older. When asked about his faith, Pasteur would reply: "The more I know, the more does my faith approach that of the Breton peasant. Could I but know all, I would have the faith of a Breton peasant woman."

Henri Fabre (1823 - 1915) was a friend of Pasteur and was also, like him, a great Christian biologist. He was a lifelong and vigorous opponent of the idea of spontaneous generation and of the entire theory of evolution. He was an observer of nature with great patience and carefulness. His studies of insects, especially in their living habitats, were unprecedented, so that he is generally considered the father of modern entomology. Fabre loved children and wrote many books on science for children.

These were very popular textbooks in French state schools until the intellectuals of the day reacted vigorously against his frequent references in them to God as the Creator and Sustainer of all things. In the later years of his life, however, like Pasteur, he received many high honors for his scientific investigations. His testimony concerning his belief in God was as follows: "Without Him I understand nothing; without Him all is darkness . . . Every period has its manias. I regard Atheism as a mania. It is the malady of the age. You could take my skin from me more easily than my faith in God."

William Thompson, Lord Kelvin (1824–1907) , was a physical scientist of the same stature as Newton and Faraday before him, and all three were Bible-believing Christians, He was an infant and teen-age prodigy and then held the chair of Natural Philosophy at the University of Glasgow for 54 years. The number of his contributions in physics and mathematics, as well as practical inventions, was enormous. He established the scale of absolute temperatures, so that such temperatures are today given as so many "degrees Kelvin." He established thermodynamics as a formal scientific discipline and formulated its first and second laws in precise terminology. He was the first scientist to adopt and use the concept of "energy."

Lord Kelvin

Joseph Lister

Lord Kelvin was a strong Christian, opposing both Lyellian uniformitarianism and Darwinian evolution. His calculation of the maximum possible age of the earth at 100 million years — far too brief for evolution — led to an extended controversy with Thomas Huxley, "Darwin's Bulldog." Modern evolutionists like to ridicule this calculation — which was based on terrestrial heat flow and the cooling of the earth — by noting that Kelvin did not know about heat from radioactivity. However, when radioactivity was discovered, Kelvin *did* consider it — and showed it would not be at all adequate to meet the need for an earth old enough to allow evolution.

Lord Kelvin also made studies which later enabled Morse to invent the telegraph. He supervised the design and laying of the first Atlantic cable, which — on top of all his other contributions — led to his being knighted and later given a barony. He held 21 honorary doctorates.

Yet with all these honors, he always remained a humble Christian, firmly believing the Bible and supporting its teaching in the schools of England. In a famous testimony given in 1903, Lord Kelvin made the unequivocal statement that, "With regard to the origin of life, science . . . positively affirms creative power."

Joseph Lister (1827 - 1912) was an English surgeon whose great contribution was the development of antiseptic surgery through the use of chemical disinfectants. This development is probably second only to Pasteur's contribution in terms of the saving of human lives. He also made notable contributions in surgery and founded what would later become the Lister Institute of Preventive Medicine in London. He was president of both the Royal Society and the British Association and was eventually raised to the peerage. Even with so many honors, he, like many other great Christian scientists, was still a humble and gracious man. Of Quaker background, Lord Lister was a firm believer throughout his life. He wrote: "I am a believer in the fundamental doctrines of Christianity."

Joseph Clerk Maxwell (1831 - 1879)   lived a short, but uniquely productive, life. One of the greatest scientists of all time, he was also a sincere Bible-believing Christian. Building on the concepts and experimental work of his friend Faraday, he developed a comprehensive theoretical and mathematical framework of electromagnetic field theory, embracing all types of energy systems (excepting gravity and nuclear forces) within the famous "electromagnetic wave spectrum." Albert Einstein called Maxwell's achievement "the most profound and most fruitful that physics has experienced since the time of Newton." He also extended classical thermodynamics into the broader field of statistical thermodynamics and made many other notable contributions in physics and mathematics.

His Christian beliefs were essentially "fundamentalist" in nature. He was strongly opposed to evolution and was able to develop a rigorous mathematical refutation of the famous "nebular hypothesis" of the French atheist LaPlace. He also wrote an incisive refutation of the evolutionary philosophies of Herbert Spencer, the great advocate of Darwinism. A prayer found in his handwriting after his death quoted the Genesis account of man's creation in God's image and the command to subdue the earth as the motivation for his own scientific studies, while also acknowledging his personal faith in Jesus Christ as Lord and Savior. He was a diligent student of the Scriptures and godly in his Christian walk.

Bernhard Riemann (1826 - 1866) was a German mathematician who developed the concept of non-Euclidean geometries. None other than Albert Einstein later developed much of his theory of relativity and space curvature on the basis of "Riemannian geometry." Riemann made other brilliant mathematical contributions, but he was also a student of theology and Biblical Hebrew. The son of a Lutheran minister, he started out studying for the ministry, until his mathematical genius diverted his studies into that field. He attempted on at least one occasion to combine the two by writing what he intended as a mathematical proof of the truth of the book of Genesis.

John Bell Pettigrew (1834 - 1908) was author of a well-known 19th century treatise on "Design in Nature," which was a real classic in this field. Even though Pettigrew allowed for evolution, He amassed a tremendous amount of evidence for design. He was one of the outstanding anatomists and physiologists of the 19th century, serving as president of the Royal Medical Society and authoring over 15 significant volumes in his disciplines.

George Romanes (1848 - 1894) was a follower and personal friend of Charles Darwin, as well as author of many books promoting evolution. He was a gifted biologist and physiologist, as well as a zealous evolutionist. But he also went through a unique pilgrimage of faith in his own life. As a student of mathematics and natural science at Cambridge, he was an ardent evangelical Christian, intending to enter the ministry. It was after his graduation that he first began to read books by Darwin and other evolutionists, and he soon lost his Christian faith and became a devoted disciple of Darwin, even writing a book against theism. As time went on, however, especially after a series of personal misfortunes, he gradually returned to his earlier faith, at least as far as his belief in the Bible and the person and work of Christ were concerned. Whether his early death occurred before he returned also to a belief in special creation is not known. However, in his last book, *Thoughts on Religion*, Romanes strongly urged his former co-agnostic friends to become true empiricists and accept Christ.

Richard Owen (1804 - 1892) was one of the strongest scientific opponents of Darwinism during the age of Darwin, writing many articles and delivering many lectures against the ideas of natural selection that were gaining currency at the time. Although he was not a Christian in the Biblical sense, he was a strong theist and supported those Christians (e.g., Bishop Wilberforce) who took a stand against Darwinism.

His scientific specialties were zoology, comparative anatomy, and paleontology. For many years he was Superintendent of the Natural History Department of the British Museum. He was the discoverer of the parathyroid glands and the first to describe the giant moas of New Zealand. He also was one of the first of the dinosaur hunters, having the distinction of coining the name *dinosaur* ("terrible lizard") and preparing the first dinosaur reconstructions for museum display. He also discovered the trichinosis parasite. He researched and wrote extensively on numerous living and extinct animals. At the time of his retirement, in 1884, he was knighted and became Sir Richard Owen.

Edward Hitchcock (1793 - 1864) was one of the first American geologists of importance, making important studies on glacial geology and serving many years as a Massachusetts state geologist. He was another man strongly influenced by Timothy Dwight, having studied under Professor Silliman. He was the first, and for twenty years the only, teacher of scientific subjects at Amherst College. From 1845 until his death, he was president of Amherst serving also as professor of geology and natural theology. During his later years he also was state geologist for Vermont. He made the first detailed study of the Connecticut River Valley.

As a Christian, he was a strong creationist and a believer in natural theology. He became probably the strongest opponent of Darwinism and evolutionism in America during his later years. He preached vigorously on the theme that belief in evolution led to atheism and the grossest materialism.

Sir Henry Rawlinson (1810 - 1895) was one of the greatest archeologists, as well as a devoted Christian and Bible student. Originally an English military man stationed in India, he is best known for his remarkable feat of exposing and deciphering the Behistun inscriptions of the Persian emperor Darius, written on the face of a great scarp in three ancient languages – Old Persian, Assyrian and Elamitic. This accomplishment opened the way to a real understanding of the ancient history of the Near and Middle East.

Sir Joseph Henry Gilbert (1817 - 1901) was one of the prominent Fellows of the Royal Society who signed the *Scientist's Declaration*, affirming his faith in the Bible as the Word of God and opposing Darwinist materialism. As an agricultural chemist, he developed nitrogen and superphosphate fertilizers for use with crops, and helped develop (as first co-director) the world's first agricultural experimental station, located in Hertfordshire in 1843. He also served as Professor of Rural Economy at Oxford University.

Thomas Anderson (1819 - 1874) was a Fellow of the Royal Society and a prominent Scotch chemist, discoverer of pyridine and other organic bases. As Regius Professor of Chemistry at Glasgow, he also edited the *Edinburgh New Philosophical Journal*. He was one of the signatories of the *Scientists' Declaration* of 1864, affirming his faith in the scientific accuracy of the Bible and the validity of the Christian faith.

Sir William Huggins (1824 - 1910) was well known as both an openly confessed Christian and a brilliant astronomer. He was the first to demonstrate from spectral studies that stars were comprised mostly of hydrogen, along with smaller amounts of the same elements existing on Earth. He was also the first to identify the Doppler effect in astronomy, leading to the idea of the expanding universe. He was a President of the Royal Society.

Balfour Stewart (1828 - 1887) was a Scottish physicist who saw no conflict between the facts of science and the fundamentals of Christianity, expressing this conviction in a number of popular writings. He is best known for his work on the magnetic field, especially the upper atmosphere electrical currents, which led to the discovery of the ionosphere.

P. G. Tait (1831 - 1901) was a Scottish physicist and mathematician who laid the foundation for vector analysis and other techniques of advanced mathematics and mathematical physics. He was professor of natural philosophy at the University of Edinburgh, and collaborated with Lord Kelvin on the development of the key concepts of energy and thermodynamics. Like Kelvin, he was widely known as an orthodox Christian of strong Biblical faith.

John Murray (1808 - 1892) , though not a scientist himself, was the head of the most important publishing firm in England, responsible for the publication of many scientific books, most notably those of Charles Lyell and Charles Darwin. He also wrote many books himself, including at least one (*Skepticism in Geology*) vigorously and effectively refuting Lyell's uniformitarianism.

James Glaisher (1809 - 1903) was for 34 years superintendent of the department of meteorology and magnetism at the Greenwich Observatory, publishing his standard dew-point tables which are still in use. He established the British Meteorological Society in 1850 and the Aeronautical Society in 1866. As a convinced Bible-believing Christian, he was one of the signers of the famous *Declaration* of 1864 (see p. 75), affirming this belief in response to the tide of Darwinism then sweeping the country.

In addition to the scientists discussed in this chapter, it is significant that 717 scientists signed a remarkable manifesto entitled "The Declaration of Students of the Natural and Physical Sciences," issued in London in 1864. This declaration affirmed their confidence in the scientific integrity of the Holy Scriptures. The list included 86 Fellows of the Royal Society. Among the more prominent signers were Brewster, Joule, Rawlinson, Sedgwick and others whose biographics are included in this book.

Chapter 7

THE MODERN PERIOD

Most of the men of science mentioned in this next section had their careers in the last years of the 19th century and the first half of the 20th century. They were separated by at least a generation from the earth-shaking careers of Darwin and his cohorts. Despite the creationist testimonies of such stellar scientists as Kelvin, Pasteur, Agassiz, Maxwell, and others, evolution's triumph was almost complete by the turn of the century. Along with evolution came liberalism, Biblical criticism, agnosticism, humanism, and atheism, not to mention communism, fascism, and social Darwinism. The universities and even most seminaries largely abandoned Biblical Christianity, and it is not surprising that the number and caliber of Christian men of science seemed to decline in this period.

Nevertheless, there were still a number of eminent scientists who did "not bow the knee to Baal," even in this desolate period.

Edward H. Maunder (1851 - 1928), for example, was a prominent British astronomer who was a

Fellow of the Royal Astronomical Society, as well as founder and president of the British Astronomical Association. He was in charge of the Solar Department of the Greenwich Observatory and probably the outstanding authority on solar astronomy of his day. He authored many books, both technical and popular, including at least one book on the astronomy of the Bible, defending the Bible's accuracy and insights in astronomical matters. He served six years as Secretary of the Victoria Institute, the venerable British society for the defense of the Christian faith.

William Mitchell Ramsay (1851 - 1939)   was among the greatest of all archeologists. A liberal in theology as a result of his university studies, he was converted to true Biblical Christianity as a result of his own uniquely extensive archeological discoveries in Asia Minor, which confirmed fully the historical statements in the book of Acts especially. He was author of over 20 books, most of which were written to provide archeological support and illumination for the New Testament. He also served as professor at Oxford and Aberdeen Universities.

John Strutt, Lord Rayleigh (1842 - 1919)   was the successor to Maxwell at Cambridge and continued his studies on the electromagnetic wave motions, making noteworthy contributions in optics, sonics, and gas dynamics. He was also the co-discoverer of argon and the rare gases. Perhaps his most significant work was in developing the important scientific tools of similitude and dimensional analysis. He was also well known as a sincere Christian believer. As a prefix to his published papers he wrote: "The works of the Lord are great, sought out of all them that have pleasure therein."

Alexander MacAlister (1844 - 1919) was Professor of Anatomy at Cambridge for many years and author of many important textbooks in zoology and physiology. He wrote this testimony: "I think the widespread impression of the agnosticism of scientific men is largely due to the attitude taken up by a few of the great popularizers of science, like Tyndall and Huxley. It has been my experience that the disbelief in the revelation that God has given in the life and work, death and resurrection of our Savior is more prevalent among what I may call the camp followers of science than amongst those to whom scientific work is the business of their lives."

A. H. Sayce (1845 - 1933) was an English philologist and archeologist whose studies contributed significantly to the vindication through archeology of the historical sections of the Old Testament. A long-time professor at Oxford, Sayce was probably the foremost Assyriologist of all time, as well as an expert on the Hittites. When he began his career, he was steeped in higher criticism, but the hard facts from the archeological and linguistic investigations in which he played a leading role contributed to his conversion to Biblical Christianity. He authored over 25 major books in his fields.

John Ambrose Fleming (1849 - 1945) could well be recognized as the father of modern electronics, devising the first true electron tube. He studied under Maxwell at Cambridge and worked as a consultant for Thomas Edison and also for Marconi. He served for over 40 years as Professor of Electrical Engineering at the University of London, receiving many honors for his contributions in electronics, radio, and television.

In addition, he was an active Christian apologist, son of a Congregational minister. He served for a time as president of the Victoria Institute and wrote at least one major book against evolution. He was also a founder and the first president of the Evolution Protest Movement.

Howard A. Kelly (1858 - 1943) was a great American Surgeon, Professor of Gynecology and Obstetrics for 22 years with the outstanding medical school at Johns Hopkins University. He was probably the number one gynecologist in America for the first two decades of this century. In addition to many authoritative book in his field, he wrote one book giving his Christian testimony, *A Scientific Man and His Bible.* Although he believed in a form of theistic evolution, he was a thorough fundamentalist otherwise and was an active soul-winning Christian.

George Washington Carver (1864 - 1943) was the great black scientist who was considered the world's top authority on peanuts and sweet potatoes and their products. Born a slave, he worked his way through college in the north and then returned to the south, desiring to devote his life to improving the quality of southern farm lands and the economic prosperity of his people. As a faculty member at the Tuskegee Institute in Alabama, he turned down a number of much more lucrative offers, as the fame of his genius as an agricultural chemist spread. IIe developed over 300 products from the peanut and over 118 from the sweet potato.

Carver was also a sincere and humble Christian, never hesitating to confess his faith in the God of the Bible and attributing all his success and ability to God. In 1939 he was awarded the Roosevelt medal, with the following citation: "To a scientist humbly seeking the guidance of God

George Washington Carver

and a liberator to men of the white race as well as the black."

Charles Stine (1882 - 1954) was for many years Director of Research for the E. I. duPont company. As an organic chemist with many degrees and honors, he developed many new products and patents for his company. He was a man of top eminence in his field, but also a simple believing Christian. He frequently spoke to scientific and university audiences concerning his faith and also wrote a small book entitled *A Chemist and His Bible*. After a stirring exposition of the gospel and an appeal to accept Christ, Dr. Stine gave this testimony of the Creator. "The world about us, far more intricate than any watch, filled with checks and balances of a hundred varieties, marvelous beyond even the imagination of the most skilled scientific investigator, this beautiful and intricate creation, bears the signature of its Creator, graven in its works."

Douglas Dewar (1875 - 1957) was a founder of the Evolution Protest Movement in London in 1932 and was a long-time leader of this organization. He had been a graduate of Cambridge in Natural Science and was an evolutionist in his early career, even authoring books on evolution. He had a distinguished career in India, both in politics and as a naturalist and ornithologist, authoring more than 20 books on the birds and the history of India. After he became a Christian and creationist, when he was about 50 years of age, he wrote numerous papers and books expounding the scientific basis of creationism. He was elected Vice President of the Victoria Institute and participated in a number of both written and oral creation/evolution debates with leading British evolutionists, including H. S. Shelton, J. B. S. Haldane, and Joseph McCabe.

Paul Lemoine (1878 - 1940) was President of the Geological Society of France, Director of the Natural History Museum in Paris, and a chief editor of the *Encyclopedie Francaise*, 1937 edition. In that work, in the article on evolution, he stated: "The theory of evolution is impossible. At base, in spite of appearances, no one any longer believes in it.... Evolution is a kind of dogma which the priests no longer believe, but which they maintain for their people." LeMoine had once been an evolutionist himself, and apparently no French scientist openly challenged the above statement at the time it was published.

William Ramsay (1852 - 1916) , well-known as an evangelical Christian chemist, was the co-discoverer of argon and the other inert gases. His discovery of terrestrial helium on the earth led him to study radioactive decay processes, and he was the first to demonstrate an actual transmutation of elements (radium into helium) by these processes. This, in turn, led him to the beginnings of what later was called isotopic chemistry by his assistant, Soddy, who then more fully developed the theory of isotopes.

Wernher von Braun (1912 - 1977) was one of the world's top space scientists. With a Ph.D. from the University of Berlin, von Braun was a leading German rocket engineer, developing the famed V-2 rocket during World War II. He migrated to the United States in 1945, becoming a naturalized U.S. citizen in 1955. He directed U.S. guided missile development for several years and then became Director of NASA.

Dr. von Braun was also a practicing Lutheran, active in church and Christian life. In the foreword to an anthology on creation and design in nature, he gave this testimony: "Manned space flight is an amazing achievement, but it has opened for mankind thus far only a tiny door for viewing the awesome reaches of space. An outlook through this peephole at the vast mysteries of the universe should only confirm our belief in the certainty of its Creator. I find it as difficult to understand a scientist who does not acknowledge the presence of a superior rationality behind the existence of the universe as it is to comprehend a theologian who would deny the advances of science."

Wernher von Braun

V-2 Rocket

Moon Walk

Sir William Abney (1843 - 1920) was the son of a clergyman and firmly believed in the harmony of science and Scripture. As president of both the Royal Astronomical Society and the Royal Physical Society, he made a number of significant studies identifying interstellar molecules through studies of spectroscopic absorption.

A. Rendle Short (1885 - 1955) was a prominent evangelical leader, active in campus evangelism and in apologetics, writing a number of excellent books in defense of the Christian faith. He was professor of surgery for many years at the University of Bristol.

L. Merson Davies (1890 - 1960), long an active participant in England's Evolution Protest Movement, was a strong conservative Christian and Bible student. He held both a Ph.D. and D. Sc. in geology and was a working geologist and paleontologist for about 30 years, publishing many significant articles in British geological journals. He participated in a number of creation/evolution debates with such leading British evolutionists as J. B. S. Haldane and others. He also published at least one widely used book defending the scientific inerrancy of the Bible.

Sir Cecil P. G. Wakeley (1892 - 1979) was President of the Evolution Protest Movement in England for 18 years, as well as President of the Bible League. He was an eminent surgeon, having served as Surgeon Rear Admiral in the Second World War, and then as Professor of Surgery in the University of London, as well as President of the Royal College of Surgeons. He received many honors in his field of science.

There were a number of other influential writers on science and the Bible during the first half of the 20th century (George McCready Price, Harry Rimmer, Byron Nelson, Arthur Brown, and others). Their scientific credentials and contributions were limited, but many of their writings were pointed, accurate, and helpful. For the most part, however, this period of modern history was more barren than others, as far as the proportions and caliber of its Bible-believing scientists were concerned. Furthermore, most theologians — even fundamentalists — were also retreating during this period, emphasizing such compromises as the "gap theory" of Genesis and focusing heavily on the "spiritual" teachings of Scripture, rather that its scientific and historical relevance. The world of science and education had been almost completely taken captive by evolutionary humanism.

Actually, though this was a scientific area, most 20th-century scientists, whether Christian or non-Christian, were of a different breed than the great pioneers of science whose careers we have been surveying. The numbers of scientists (all indoctrinated in evolutionism in their schooling) had increased astronomically, but perhaps not in quality or dedication. Large teams of scientists now worked on government-sponsored projects, often of doubtful significance. Each person tended to become highly specialized on various minutia of science, and the number and caliber of real breakthroughs, new fields, and broad discoveries truly benefiting mankind were not nearly so great as there once had been, even though the technological level of society continued to advance.

This fact makes the high correlation of such breakthroughs with the names of the great Bible-believing scientists of the past seem even more significant. These data are summarized in partial fashion in the Appendix. Until this present century, the entire scientific enterprise was still being conducted against a background of at least a nominal Christian world view, with its concepts of rationality and purpose in nature, along with the implication of man's stewardship of nature under God. Even non-Christian scientists held similar views to those of Christians in regard to their responsibilities as scientists, and this environment stimulated a spirit of dedication and meaningfulness to science, which began to dissipate with the triumph of humanistic and existentialist world views in the 20th century.

Chapter 8

THE REVIVAL OF CREATIONISM

The discouraging situation of the early decades of this century is now going through a dramatic change. Instead of only a handful of Bible-believing scientists, there are now thousands. Several factors have contributed to this, but probably the most significant has been the modern revival of creationism, not merely as a religious belief, but as a serious scientific alternative to evolution. In any case, the fact is that now, in every field of science, there can be found a significant and growing number of men and women who believe the Bible and are evangelical, witnessing Christians. Some of these may consider themselves theistic evolutionists or progressive creationists, but there are thousands who are unashamed literal creationists, believing that all things were created and made in the six solar days described in the first chapter of Genesis.

Most of these people were educated in humanistic, evolutionary schools, and so have come to their convictions the hard way. They are familiar with all arguments against the

Bible and special creation and have had to refute these argument in their own thinking first of all. They are each convinced that, in their own fields of science, the real facts support the Bible and their Christian faith. Many have suffered one or another form of persecution for their stand, and yet they *stand!*

We have been giving brief biographies of some of the great Christian scientists of the past. However, it would not be appropriate to try at this point to do the same for scientists who are still living. Some would not wish to be mentioned, while others might be inadvertently omitted who *should* have been included. Furthermore, none of them have yet completed their careers, so it would be premature to compare any of them with scientists of previous generations. Consequently, we can only refer to groups of living scientists, rather than naming them individually.

The **Creation Research Society** is undoubtedly the most significant such group. Organized in 1963 by ten scientists, it soon grew to a regular membership of over 700 (scientists with one or more post-graduate degrees in a pure or applied natural science), plus about 2,000 sustaining members. All members subscribe to a doctrinal statement which embraces the inspiration of the Bible, the deity and substitutionary atonement of Christ, and the historicity of the Genesis record of special six-day creation and the worldwide cataclysmic flood.

The **American Scientific Affiliation** is somewhat smaller than the **CRS**, in terms of credentialed scientific members, though comparable in total membership. It was formed by six scientists in 1944. Its original statement of faith was later modified considerably and its philosophical spectrum broadened. It is now predominantly composed of theistic evolutionists and progressive creationists, but there are still many members who believe in Biblical inerrancy and the authority of Christ and the gospel.

The **Bible-Science Association** was organized in 1963, soon after the **CRS**. It is primarily an organization of concerned laymen, but does contain a sprinkling of scientists who are not members of the **CRS**, as well as many who are. Its doctrinal position is quite similar to that of **CRS**.

The **Institute for Creation Research** is unique in that it is not a membership society, but an actual educational institution, with an excellent staff of scientists dedicated to promoting scientific and Biblical creationism through a threefold program of research, writing, and teaching. It was organized in 1970 and has a current staff (as of 1988) was organized in 1970 and has a current staff (as of 1988) of nine full-time and several part-time scientists, plus about 22 others who serve as regional representatives, advisory board members, or trustees. All of these have at least a terminal degree or equivalent in some relevant natural science, pure or applied. The doctrinal position is similar to that of **CRS**, though considerably more specific. **ICR** also has produced about 70 books and monographs and offers a wide range of extension programs. Its educational ministries include a graduate school offering M.S. degree programs in several key areas of science.

There are at least 100 other smaller creationist organizations, both national and local, as well as foreign.

We trust the material in this book has made it abundantly clear that the frequent claims to the effect that no true scientist could believe the Bible – especially the book of Genesis – are ridiculously wrong. There have been and presently are many thousands of such believing scientists, including many of the greatest scientists of all time. This fact certainly does not *prove* the Bible (the Bible can speak for itself), but perhaps it will help put these unwarranted claims of skeptics in their proper perspective.

In the meantime, the reader is urged to begin a renewed study of the Bible in light of its assured scientific integrity. For those who are not already committed Christian believers, the step of scientific empiricism is earnestly recommended. That is: "Commit thy way unto the Lord; trust also in Him; and He shall bring it to pass" (Psalm 37:5). "These things have I written unto you that believe on the name of the Son of God; that ye may know that ye have eternal life" (I John 5:13).

Appendix

Key Contributions of Bible-believing Scientists of the Past

Scientist	Discipline founded or developed; discovery, invention, or other key contribution
Leonardo da Vinci (1452 - 1519)	Experimental science; Physics
Francis Bacon (1561 - 1626)	Scientific method
Johann Kepler (1571 - 1630)	Scientific astronomy
William Petty (1623 - 1687)	Statistics; Scientific economics
Blaise Pascal (1623 - 1662)	Hydrostatics; Barometer
Robert Boyle (1627 - 1691)	Chemistry; Gas dynamics
John Ray (1627 - 1705)	Natural history
Nicolas Steno (1631 - 1686)	Stratigraphy
Isaac Newton (1642 - 1727)	Dynamics; Calculus; Gravitation law; Reflecting telescope
William Derham (1657 - 1735)	Ecology
John Woodward (1665 - 1728)	Paleontology
Carolus Linneaus (1707 - 1778)	Taxonomy; Biological classification system
Richard Kirwan (1733 - 1812)	Mineralogy
William Herschel (1738 - 1822)	Galactic astronomy; Uranus
John Dalton (1766 - 1844)	Atomic theory; Gas law
Georges Cuvier (1769 - 1832)	Comparative anatomy
Humphrey Davy (1778 - 1829)	Thermokinetics; Safety lamp

John Kidd, M.D. (1775 - 1851)	Chemical synthetics
David Brewster (1781 - 1868)	Optical mineralogy; Kaleidoscope
William Prout (1785 - 1850)	Food chemistry
Michael Faraday (1791 - 1867)	Electro magnetics; Field theory; Generator
Charles Babbage (1792 - 1871)	Operations research; Computer science; Opthalmoscope
Samuel F. B. Morse (1791 - 1872)	Telegraph
William Whewell (1794 - 1866)	Anemometer
Joseph Henry (1797 - 1878)	Electric motor; Galvanometer
Matthew Maury (1806 - 1873)	Oceanography; Hydrography
Louis Agassiz (1807 - 1873)	Glaciology; Ichthyology
James Simpson (1811 - 1870)	Gynecology; Anesthesiology
James Joule (1818 - 1889)	Thermodynamics
George Stokes (1819 - 1903)	Fluid Mechanics
Rudolph Virchow (1821 - 1902)	Pathology
Louis Pasteur (1822 - 1895)	Bacteriology; Biochemistry; Sterilization; Immunization
Gregor Mendel (1822 - 1884)	Genetics
Henri Fabre (1823 - 1915)	Entomology of living insects
William Thompson, Lord Kelvin (1824 - 1907)	Energetics; Absolute temperatures; Atlantic cable
William Huggins (1824 - 1910)	Astral spectrometry
Bernhard Riemann (1826 - 1866)	Non-Euclidean geometrics
Joseph Lister (1827 - 1912)	Antiseptic surgery
Balfour Stewart (1828 - 1887)	Ionospheric electricity

Joseph Clerk Maxwell (1831 - 1879)	Electrodynamics; Statistical thermodynamics
P. G. Tait (1831 - 1901)	Vector analysis
John Strutt, Lord Rayleigh (1842 - 1919)	Similitude; Model Analysis; Inert Gases
John Ambrose Fleming (1849 - 1945)	Electronics; Electron tube; Thermionic valve
William Ramsay (1852 - 1916)	Isotopic chemistry, Element transmutation

Index

Modern Creation Trilogy

Volume I - Scripture and Creation
Volume II - Science and Creation
Volume III - Society and Creation

Dr. Henry M. Morris
and Dr. John D. Morris

The definitive work on the study of origins, from a creationist perspective, *The Modern Creation Trilogy* examines the evidences for both evolution and special creation. Authored by the prolific father-son research team of Henry and John Morris, this three-volume gift set is a "must-have" for those who believe the Bible is God's plain-spoken Word.

Volume I looks at what the Bible says about origins — man, animal, planet, and universe. Volume II studies the scientific evidences for evolution and creation, contending that the evidence favors creation, since none of us were there in the beginning. Volume III sheds light on the fruits of each worldview — which stance produces better results for all creation? Interest level: Adult.. CD Rom included.

ISBN: 0-89051-216-7
Gift-boxed set of three • Paperback • 5-1/4 x 8-1/2 • $44.95